SELECTED POEMS

BY THE SAME AUTHOR

POETRY

The hoop
Common Knowledge
Feast Days
The Myth of the Twin
Swimming in the Flood
A Normal Skin
The Asylum Dance
The Light Trap
The Good Neighbour

FICTION

The Dumb House
The Mercy Boys
Burning Elvis
The Locust Room
Living Nowhere

NON-FICTION

A Lie About My Father

SELECTED POEMS

John Burnside

CAPE POETRY

Published by Jonathan Cape 2006

2 4 6 8 10 9 7 5 3 1

Copyright © John Burnside 2006

John Burnside has asserted his right under the Copyright, Designs
and Patents Act 1988 to be identified as the author of this work

This book is sold subject to the condition that it shall not,
by way of trade or otherwise, be lent, resold, hired out,
or otherwise circulated without the publisher's prior
consent in any form of binding or cover other than that
in which it is published and without a similar condition
including this condition being imposed on the
subsequent purchaser

First published in Great Britain in 2006 by
Jonathan Cape
Random House, 20 Vauxhall Bridge Road, London SW1V 2SA

Random House Australia (Pty) Limited
20 Alfred Street, Milsons Point, Sydney,
New South Wales 2061, Australia

Random House New Zealand Limited
18 Poland Road, Glenfield,
Auckland 10, New Zealand

Random House South Africa (Pty) Limited
Isle of Houghton, Corner Boundary Road & Carse O'Gowrie,
Houghton 2198, South Africa

The Random House Group Limited Reg. No. 954009
www.randomhouse.co.uk

A CIP catalogue record for this book is
available from the British Library

ISBN 0-224-07803-8

Papers used by Random House are natural,
recyclable products made from wood grown in sustainable forests;
the manufacturing processes conform to the environmental
regulations of the country of origin

Typeset in Bembo by Palimpsest Book Production Limited, Polmont, Stirlingshire
Printed and bound in Great Britain by William Clowes Ltd, Beccles, Suffolk

*E allora? Eppure resta
che qualcosa è accaduto, forse un niente
che è tutto.*

Eugenio Montale, 'Xenia II'

for Sarah, Lucas and Gil

CONTENTS

from *Common Knowledge* (1991)

'Like me, you sometimes waken'	1
Suburbs	2
Signal Stop, near Horsley	7

from *Feast Days* (1992)

Septuagesima	8
Lost	9
8 a.m. near Chilworth	10

from *Myth of the Twin* (1994)

Halloween	11
Pisces	12
Dialect	13
The Pit Town in Winter	14
The Solitary in Autumn	15

from *Swimming in the Flood* (1995)

Swimming in the Flood	16
Catch-Kiss	18
A Swimming Lesson	19
Burning a Woman	22
Natalie	27

from *A Normal Skin* (1997)

A Normal Skin	28
Snake	30
from Epithalamium	31
Penitence	39

from *The Asylum Dance* (2000)

Ports	41
Settlements	49
The Asylum Dance	56
Fields	59
Husbandry	69
Roads	70

from *The Light Trap* (2002)

Koi	82
Animals	85
Heat Wave	87
History	89
After Lucretius	92

from *The Good Neighbour* (2005)

The Good Neighbour	100
Haar	101
Homage to Kåre Kivijärvi	104
The Last Man to Speak Ubykh	105
The Painter Fabritius Begins Work on the Lost *Noli Me Tangere* of 1652	107

Like me, you sometimes waken
early in the dark
thinking you have driven miles
through inward country,

feeling around you still
the streaming trees and startled waterfowl
and summered cattle
swinging through your headlamps.

Sometimes you linger days
upon a word,
a single, uncontaminated drop
of sound; for days

it trembles, liquid to the mind,
then falls:
mere denotation,
dimming in the undertow of language.

SUBURBS

Wet Sunday afternoon; after the rain a bible wind ripples the sheet puddles on Station Road; along the hedges by the girls' school an elaborate birdsong streams through the wet scent of roses, like a new form of music evolving out of water.

The spiritual history of the suburb: Dutch paintings of parrots and cockatoos, Chinese damasks, Kraak porcelains, still-lifes of spices and fruits, imported rhubarb, ginger, cochineal; bottles of gherkins and maple syrup on kitchen tables, ice-cream and lemons, radios talking to empty rooms, the way they do when the director is aiming for suspense in a fifties murder film – the suburb always has an abstracted quality, like a sentence learned by heart and repeated till the words are finally magical.

At night the suburb alters. The day-long, low-level action beneath the surface intensifies, like bad wood warping under veneer: the garden is stolen by foxes rooting in turned dustbins, emptiness takes form and approaches from the centre of the lawn, a white devil, smiling out of the dark, and the realisation dawns that I live in an invented place whose only purpose is avoidance, and what I would avoid, I carry with me, always.

We used to walk in the suburbs, spying into the houses of people we imagined were rich: interiors of perfect stillness, unbearably tidy; Imari bowls and baby grand pianos; gloves on hall tables; mirrors; paintings of boats and landscapes – the people, the trimmed lapdogs, even the space in the middle of each room seemed nothing other than an additional item of furniture, capable of being polished and insured.

In winter the suburb is Japanese. It is quiet and formal: stone tables and cryptomerias stand in the fenced yards, in tightly-stitched sleeves of immaculate snow. Nevertheless, something is missing: an absence that is only temporarily filled by the red of a post van in the lane, or the sound of footsteps crunching ice. At the edge of the wood, beyond what might reasonably be called suburb, on the already mythical rim of countryside, a pillar-box stands in a drift of the same whiteness, filling its space with a colour and solidity the suburb cannot emulate.

For this reason, the last true rituals only happen here: the inhabitants of the suburb are compelled by an attention to detail that was once religious and is now quite meaningless. The suburb has its own patterns: arrangements of bottles on front steps and scraped ice on driveways, enactments of chores and duties, conversations at gates and hedges, sweeping and binding movements, arcane calculations of cost and distance. All this activity is intended to make it appear real – a commonplace – but its people cannot evade the thought, like the thought which sometimes comes in dreams, that nothing is solid at all, and the suburb is no more substantial than a mirage in a blizzard, or the shimmering waves off an exit road where spilled petrol evaporates in the sun.

The recurring dream is also a memory: I step from the smoke and noise of a party in the suburbs, into a cool garden that smells of lilies and nicotiana; the stars are close, sparkling, cold, and I want to reach up and brush my fingers over their points. In one step I rise into the top branches of an apple tree, into the damp and the perfume, where a girl in a white dress is already standing, half in darkness, half in the light, lily-scented, as if she belonged to the garden, and could emerge and melt back into it at will.

There is no need to speak; each of us hears the other's thoughts; through the music and voices they all run together, not just sounds, but scents and scraps of vision: lights, moths, perfumes, tunnels, streams. Half ideas: the notation of a tendency towards the circular, a neatness I have known about for years, expressed in a strange algebra of place names and symbols on road maps.

After a while, in the dream and the memory, she is gone. I walk back indoors and the kitchen is empty, except for an absence where something has just occupied my place and left a glass of milk half-finished on the table, some angel of weights and measures who passed through and has only just left – I hear its engine running in the dark, a shining configuration of old gods, Pan–Shiva, Persephone–Ishtar, the Janus–Christ of thresholds and crossings, the imprint of a child who has never come indoors and never will, who stays out in all weathers, who will never grow up or die, who is always, in all circumstances, *out to play.*

In the late afternoon, the people indoors; catspaws of light on the honeydew leaves, sprinklers surging and hissing on deserted lawns. A mile away the abandoned railway station is buried in grapevine and cherry laurel, already half-surrendered to the woods, like a temple to some forgotten god; a half mile in the other direction, stone crosses and angels stand wrapped in graveyard lichens, lithe muscle snakes in ivy, water drips all evening from a rusting tap; this is another form of the same greenness, quieter, more familiar, but what makes it beautiful is what makes it dangerous, like the spirit of the fish pool which flares out and taints our children.

Sometimes I am beguiled by its most primitive identity: a place where I can grow plants; a warm kitchen where I can sit undisturbed, listening for the milk and the post, while the sun rises behind the apple tree and tissues of risen water stream in the grass beyond my boundary. Sometimes its simplicity is deception: the distance arrives in a thread of cool perfume between two curtains, and I think I am already present somewhere else, having made a journey of some kind, as if any journey could end somewhere other than here, in the suburbs, where everything is implied: city, warehouse district, night stop, woods emerging from mists, as if newly-created, like those Japanese paper flowers which unfold in water, empty back roads at night where, momentarily, a soughing of wings passes close in the dark, followed by the tug of silence, the feel of grain fields shifting under the wind, a lamp in a window beyond, where someone has sat up all night, drinking tea, remembering something like this.

The suburb accumulates accidents: books on topology or nomadism that looked interesting in the shop; overgrown gardens of mint and anchusa; out-buildings littered with clay shards and clotted rags, like the floor of an Egyptian tomb. Thick black liquors remain for years under the rims of jamjars and lemonade bottles, like fairy-tale recipes for invisibility or love.

Place is not important; even if the details are beguiling, the night is what matters: the constant of night in Chantilly or Cherry Hinton, a night that could be populated with creatures from Grünewald or Richard Dadd, but instead is revealed as the sinister playful kinship of everyday objects: wet lawns, dark hedges, cats walking on fence rims and plump, silent carp in fish ponds that might have been painted by Hiroshige; the scent of tobacco plants, the sweetness of my own mouth, a warmth moving on my skin, a sensation on my scalp of surfacing, now and always, into the moment.

I wake at night and hear someone moving in the dark, near the bed, or I see, quite clearly in the moonlight, a thin, malicious or joyful child who once belonged to me but has now gone over to collaborate in the being of those scavenger angels who haunt the suburbs, unconcerned with the notion that this space, with its locked doors and drawn blinds, belongs to my simple idea of order, which is nothing more than a notion of worthwhile and calculable risk.

SIGNAL STOP, NEAR HORSLEY

Smoke in the woods
like someone walking in a silent film
beside the tracks.

A shape I recognise – not smoke, or not just smoke,
and not just snow on hazels
or fox-trails from the platform to the trees,

but winter, neither friend
nor stranger, like the girl I sometimes glimpse

at daybreak near the crossing, in a dress
of sleet and berries, gazing at the train.

SEPTUAGESIMA

'Nombres.
Están sobre la pátina
de las cosas.'
(Jorge Guillén)

I dream of the silence
the day before Adam came
to name the animals,

the gold skins newly dropped
from God's bright fingers, still
implicit with the light.

A day like this, perhaps:
a winter whiteness
haunting the creation,

as we are sometimes
haunted by the space
we fill, or by the forms

we might have known
before the names,
beyond the gloss of things.

LOST

The wood where I was gone
for ages, on those Sunday afternoons:

lost on purpose, looking for the lithe
weasel in the grass,

stopped in my tracks, the way you stop
for echoes. Gone into the cool

of summer, passing the line
where sunlight snagged in the nettles,

I wanted the pink-toothed
killer, the casual

expert, the tribal memory of one
who slips into the chicken runs of mind

and works his way with something of my own
bright rage towards the folly of the damned.

8 A.M. NEAR CHILWORTH

Something has crossed the fields,
a series of claw prints
filling with plum-coloured water;

the stations run for miles:
a single whiteness threaded to the sun;
out in the woods

song-thrushes shiver the snow
from hazels, and the after-stain
of vixen is an echo from the book

of stories children tell on journeys home:
half-disbelieving, fingering the glass,
matching each flake of snow with inward brightness.

HALLOWEEN

I have peeled the bark from the tree
to smell its ghost,
and walked the boundaries of ice and bone
where the parish returns to itself
in a flurry of snow;

I have learned to observe the winters:
the apples that fall for days
in abandoned yards,
the fernwork of ice and water
sealing me up with the dead
in misted rooms

as I come to define my place:
barn owls hunting in pairs along the hedge,
the smell of frost on the linen, the smell of leaves
and the whiteness that breeds in the flaked
leaf mould, like the first elusive threads
of unmade souls.

The village is over there, in a pool of bells,
and beyond that nothing,
or only the other versions of myself,
familiar and strange, and swaddled in their time
as I am, standing out beneath the moon
or stooping to a clutch of twigs and straw
to breathe a little life into the fire.

PISCES

She loved the wet whisper of silt
when tidewater seeped away
and the estuary rose to the town
through copper light,

a tender of glass and scales
and driftwood varnished with salt,
a circle she walked for miles
in search of shells,

picking starfish from a sheet
of silver tension, puzzled by the trails
of viscera, the threads of bloodless meat
and resurrected forms that had no names

but offered kinship, memory, regret,
a pulse between the water and her hand,
the feel of something old and buried deep,
heartbeat and vision quickening the sand.

DIALECT

There were different words for dust:
one for the powdered film
of shading on a closed room's
windowsills,

and one for the inch-thick
layer of talcum and fibre
under the bed,

but nothing to describe the vividness
of rain-dark fur and flesh that shaped and gloved
the body of a fox beside the road,

and nothing for the presence still to come,
when wind and sunlight fretted at the bone,
cutting towards the basics of the form:
the knitted spine, the hunter's steady grin.

THE PIT TOWN IN WINTER

Everything would vanish in the snow,
fox bones and knuckles of coal
and dolls left out in the gardens,
red-mouthed and nude.

We shovelled and swept the paths,
but they melted away in the night
and the cars stood buried and dumb
on Fulford Road.

We might as well be lost, she said;
but I felt the neighbours dreaming in the dark,
and saw them wrapped in overcoats and scarves
on Sundays: careful, narrow-footed souls,
become the creatures of a sudden light,
amazed at how mysterious they were.

THE SOLITARY IN AUTUMN

I am standing out in the yard
at the end of October,
building a fire of drifted leaves and twigs,
letters for kindling, apples amongst the flames,
the last of summer, dropping through the embers.

There is that perfume in the shade
that is almost viburnum,
traces of snow and water in the light,
a blankness along the canal
that waits to be filled

and, given the silence, given the promise of frost,
I might have welcomed this as something else:
the taste of windfalls moving on the stream
a faint god's partial emergence
through willow and alder.

The riverbank darkens and fades.
The garden recovers its creatures: slow worms and frogs
and blackbirds sifting the dead
in the still of the damsons.
Across the river, evening bleeds the trees,

my neighbour's garden blurs to smoke and rain;
sometimes I think that someone else is there,
standing in his own yard, raking leaves,
or bending to a clutch of twigs and straw
to breathe a little life into the fire.

SWIMMING IN THE FLOOD

Later he must have watched
the newsreel,

his village erased by water: farmsteads and churches
breaking and floating away

as if by design;
bloated cattle, lumber, bales of straw,

turning in local whirlpools; the camera
panning across the surface, finding the odd

rooftop or skeletal tree,
or homing in to focus on a child's

shock-headed doll.
Under it all, his house would be standing intact,

the roses and lime trees, the windows,
the baby grand.

He saw it through the water when he dreamed
and, waking at night, he remembered the rescue boat,

the chickens at the prow, his neighbour's pig,
the woman beside him, clutching a silver frame,

her face dislodged, reduced to a puzzle of bone
and atmosphere, the tremors on her skin

wayward and dark, like shadows crossing a field
of clouded grain.

Later, he would see her on the screen,
trying to smile, as they lifted her on to the dock,

and he'd notice the frame again, baroque and absurd,
and empty, like the faces of the drowned.

CATCH-KISS

A scrap of memory: I'm six years old,
it's dark, it's hot, there's someone in my room.
I'm rubbing out the man I used to draw,
the clubfoot at the corner of the page
with scary eyes.
I'm rubbing out the interrupted park,
that no-man's-land beyond the public baths,
its cinemas and minor industries,
buttonmakers, chapels of repose.
His hands are cold. He makes me close my eyes
then lift my skirt and promise not to tell.
I'm eight years old. It's warm. The sun's too bright.
I'm rubbing out the girl I used to draw,
her awkward love, her feigned incompetence.
I've found a better colour for her dress,
a blue in the middle-distance that might be fog,
an endless four o'clock of light and snow.
I fill the house with robins' eggs and stars,
yellow ochre, jars of sticklebacks.
You'll find them in the picture: faded stains,
traces, relics, shreds of understanding.
Sometimes he held my face and made me drink.
His friend was there. He said I'd been asleep.
I've found a place for mother in the yard:
you'll see her later, standing by the tree.
I'll draw this girl again: her yellow dress,
her way of staying hidden till the last.
I'll draw the room, an attic in the roof
where someone else – a girl I ought to know –
is calling softly, crying in the dark,
waiting to be released
from her buckled sleeves.

A SWIMMING LESSON

Maybe it's luck, or a talent for going naked
that lets one body mingle with the stream
till fingers and eyes and even the lungs
are water. Maybe it's a gift
for transformation,
changing from child to swan at the river's edge,
from swan to fish, from fish to waterweed.
And maybe it's a pledge to gravity
that keeps another wedded to the earth,
the way I would dive to prove the riverbed
before I could swim midstream,
probing the mud with my fingers, clawing up handfuls
of pebbles and silt, and drowned bodies
eased from their bones
– I had to know that solid ground was there,
while she was drifting, merging with the tide,
taking a form from the water and making it hers,
accepting its favours, repaying the debt in kind.

In my dream you are sitting out
at the edge of the water,
watching me wade towards you in the dark:
time has stood still since the river
leached out the last thread of warmth and left you to dry,
the blue of your lips, the strawberry-red of your mouth,
a lure for the boys who found you, a lifetime away.
In my dream I am lifting the eyes from your milky skull
and I'm placing these pebbles of glass in the empty sockets
to see if they'll quicken and heal in your salvaged flesh.

She lived at the far end of town.
After the lesson, she'd leave me and wander away
through coal-black woods beyond the railway yards

where men and dogs were hunting in the grass,
drawing their secret kills from a web of static.
I never went that far, I always stopped,
though sometimes I thought I was there, in my scarf and gloves,
standing out under an elm tree, watching the shadows
flare from my torch beam, up in the higher boughs.
There were houses out there, there were rooms filled with spiders and damp
where children could go for a dare and be unreturned,
– empty blouses, sandals, cotton socks –
and ten yards into the bushes, a holy well
that was only a puddle of mud and clouded rain,
where Ellen MacInnes was brushed by a sand-coloured wing
and wandered home pregnant.

Waiting for you to step
like a heron out of the slow
green river,
I watched the reed beds
darken with a long caressing wind,
and wondered what we leave
beneath the silt,
footprints and tangles of hair
that will sink forever,
that bracelet you once let fall
through the streaming weeds
– diving for almost an hour, we came up
empty-handed, feeling it settle and drift,
like the bodies we shed
when we hoist ourselves on to the bank,
moving away for good
in a skin's depth of water.

She swam in the dark and the light,
but midnight was what she knew
like the warp of her mind,
the cattle gathered round to watch her rise,
the smell of the trees, the leaf-melt that clung to her fingers
– so it was dawn when they found her
somewhere downriver,
a nakedness for everyone to share,
boys on the footpath,
policemen with hooks and lines
– and I'd choose to remember
a country of mile-deep woods,
shoals of fishes hanging in the streams
like coloured flags, and my shadow swimming away
on a field of barley,
but all I can see is the mud in the lines of her face,
and the scatter of leaves
that someone has brushed aside,
revealing the clouded skin, and the gas-blue eyes
where thinking has stopped,
like the calm at the edge of a snowfall.

BURNING A WOMAN

I WITCH WIFE

Sooner or later, you know she will make a spell
to feel the devil simmer in her flesh,

the moment of her pleasure incandescent:
foreign spirits burning in the dark

while others sleep. A woman in the house
is partly a hostage to fortune

and partly your mirror
shaken and brought to life

and no matter how often you try
to draw the thread of brightness from a son's

water and buttermilk skin,
his mother's language trickles off his tongue

and he stands in the yard like a girl
while you bring in the cattle,

snuffling and giggling,
calling each heifer by name.

II CARDIAC

My father is standing tall
in our narrow kitchen:

blood on the table,
a litter of eggs and glass

on the clouded floor.
He's clutching a fistful of coins

like a drowning swimmer,
drunk again, and dead these seven years,

but still, in my frightened dreams,
immersed in anger;

looking for someone to blame
that he might be pardoned

and go down under the flood
with his heart intact.

III A PINT OF MILD

I liked how he said it, as if it were
honey, or dew,
or something you drank with the ladies:
a secret pleasure.
It made me believe he had come
from another language,
with names for the colour of pines
in the morning sun
or how a woman smells when giving birth,
and no historic past
or future tense,
only a present of streetlamps and empty roads,
and men spilling out of the light, in the evening air,
or wandering into the blue
of a different story.

IV LIKE FATHER

Let me imagine you capable of love
and transformation,

the dream of a man made subtle, or straight as a die,
a judge of character, a connoisseur,

whatever you thought you had lost, when you made me
listen for years to stories I couldn't believe.

I know how you shift and start when I'm passing the time,
walking from church to church in a foreign city,

making coffee, talking on the phone,
clumsy, helpless, sorry for myself,

and just the man you wanted me to be,
good for nothing, skilled in self-deceit,

punished so often for errors I never made
I'm blind to my worst mistakes, and beyond redemption.

V BURNING A WOMAN

A dark afternoon. The houses on Eastwood Road
are Belgian, all of a sudden,
where someone has lit a fire in a corner of privet;

damp and slow, a fleece of yellow smoke
clings to the leaves like mildew; I think of the time
my father stood in the yard at Handcross Court

burning my mother, a fortnight after she died:
her only coat, her witch's broom of scarves,
bonnets and nylons, ribbons of freshwater pearls.

I've worked from this faded blueprint and got it wrong
time after time,
thinking I see him wandering back and forth,

trailing dresses, stoking the fire with shoes
to watch them burn,
then seeing myself, next morning in the rain,

probing the ashes for salvage, for hairpins and beads,
a litter of buttons, like eggs going cold in the nest,
or the précis of stitchwork and feathers she once made good.

NATALIE

I

She wanted a house in the country
near Stonham Parva:
a pink house, with birds in the garden,
junipers, beehives, a horseshoe to hang on the door.
She would marry in haste.
She wanted a car she could drive
to Ipswich, or Yarmouth,
glimpses of alien lives
through a living-room window
and, later, the absolute cold
of the possible ghost,
where attic lights were golden in the dark,
and distant, like beauty, or love, or a sense of herself,
almost impossible, always about to begin.

II

She bled through the noise of the sea.
A last hour of pain and dismay
on a public beach.
The endless stars, the wonder of it all,
the taste of salt, the pebbles in her coat
dwindling away, as a stranger took what he wanted,
then more, and left her
boneless in the sand.
At dawn she was found near the pier
by a man and his dog,
blue as a jellyfish, maculate, stripped to the waist,
looking as if there was something she wanted to say,
her mouth struck open, choking on the gag,
smudged with detergent, blood-bruises, blisters of laver.

A NORMAL SKIN

The wet days come like a rash:
after a month of sun, the windowpanes
are clouded with the afterlife
of cat fur and busy-lizzies,
and, gloved in her latest attack
of eczema, our silent neighbour
sits between her curtains like a burning
candle, her face turned aside,
her shoulders hunched.
She's taking apart the clocks she collected all year
at boot fairs and local fêtes
and laying them out in pieces on the table.
She knows how things are made – that's not the point –
what matters is the order she creates
and fixes in her mind:
a map of cogs and springs, laid out in rows,
invisibly numbered.
                What we desire in pain
is order, the impression of a life
that cannot be destroyed, only dismantled.
For years you would buy those razors with orange handles,
the toothpastes and mild shampoos for a sensitive skin
I never had. For years, I took apart
the memories I thought would make me whole
being unravelled.
                What we desire in pain
is reason: an impression of ourselves
as wounded, explained,
coerced from a destination.
                Late at night,
our neighbour draws her curtains, disappears,
and lies in the healing darkness, half-awake,
achieving a normal skin

by an effort of will.
                         I'm not the one you thought
was sensitive, the soul you hoped to find:
arriving home, still wet with moonlit rain,
I enter the silence you left, in a dreamless house,
and reckon how little I feel,
when I stop to listen.

SNAKE

As cats bring their smiling
mouse-kills and hypnotised birds,
slinking home under the light
of a summer's morning
to offer the gift of a corpse,

you carry home the snake you thought
was sunning itself on a rock
at the river's edge:
sun-fretted, gracile,
it shimmies and sways in your hands
like a muscle of light,
and you gather it up like a braid
for my admiration.

I can't shake the old wife's tale
that snakes never die,
they hang in a seamless dream
of frogskin and water,
preserving a ribbon of heat
in a bone or a vein,
a cold-blooded creature's
promise of resurrection,

and I'm amazed to see you shuffle off
the woman I've know for years,
tracing the lithe, hard body, the hinge of the jaw,
the tension where sex might be, that I always assume
is neuter, when I walk our muffled house
at nightfall, throwing switches, locking doors.

from EPITHALAMIUM

Da kam ich auf einen breiten Weg;
da kam ein Engelein und wollt' mich abweisen.
Ach nein! Ich ließ mich nicht abweisen!

(Des Knaben Wunderhorn)

I SHEKINAH

I've heard how the trawlermen harvest
quivering, sexless fish
from the ache of the sea;
how they stand on the lighted decks and hold
the clouded bodies,
watching the absence form in those buttoned eyes
and thinking of their children, home in bed,
their songless wives, made strange by years of dreaming.
I've heard that seal-folk drift in from the haar
through open doors,
the cold that strokes your lips while I am gone,
probing your sleep and stealing a little warmth
to mimic love
– so, driving back, it's always a surprise
that coming home is only to the given:
old gardens in Lochgelly, thick with privet;
still-pools of oil and silt at Pittenweem;
lights on the Isle of May; the low woods
filling with salted rain beyond Markinch.
It's always a surprise: the stink of neeps;
the malt-spills of autumn fields, where floodlit tractors
labour and churn;
the last few miles of wind and scudding clouds,
or starlit silence, hung around the house,

as vivid as the angel who attends
all marriages.
                Its shimmer on our bed
is subtle, but it keeps us to itself,
learning the make-believe of granted love,
and this is all we know, an angel's gift:
that weddings are imagined, love's contrived
while each of us has one more tale to tell,
the way you feel the turning of the tide
beneath the house, or somewhere in the roof,
or how I sometimes linger on the stairs,
listening for nothing, unconvinced,
less husband than accomplice to the dark,
beguiled by the pull of the moon
and the leylines of herring.

II HEIMWEH

Remembering the story of a man
who left the village one bright afternoon,
wandering out in his shirt-sleeves and never returning,
I walk in this blur of heat to the harbour wall,
and sit with my hands in my pockets, gazing back
at painted houses, shopfronts, narrow roofs,
people about their business, neighbours, tourists,
the gaunt men loading boats with lobster creels,
women in hats and coats, despite the sun,
walking to church and gossip.
It seems too small, too thoroughly contained,
the quiet affliction of home and its small adjustments,
dogs in the backstreets, barking at every noise,
tidy gardens, crammed with bedding plants.
I turn to the grey of the sea and the further shore:
the thought of distance, endless navigation,
and wonder where he went, that quiet husband,
leaving his keys, his money,
his snow-blind life. It's strange how the ones who vanish
seem weightless and clean, as if they have stepped away
to the near-angelic.
The clock strikes four. On the sea wall, the boys from the village
are stripped to the waist and plunging in random pairs
to the glass-smooth water;
they drop feet first, or curl their small, hard bodies to a ball
and disappear for minutes in the blue.
It's hard not to think this moment is all they desire,
the best ones stay down longest, till their friends
grow anxious, then they re-emerge
like cormorants, some yards from where they dived,
renewing their pact with the air, then swimming back
to start again. It's endlessly repeatable, their private game,
exclusive, pointless, wholly improvised.

I watch them for a while, then turn for home,
made tentative, half-waiting for the day
I lock my door for good, and leave behind
the smell of fish and grain, your silent fear,
our difficult and unrelenting love.

III AFTER THE STORM

The wind has sealed our house with a thin
layer of dust;
study the landing windows and you'll find
tiny particles of leaf and shell,
insect bodies, crystals of salt and mica.
The radio's playing; you've put the kettle on
and, standing in your winter coat and gloves,
you listen to that song you've always liked,
the one about love.
Somewhere outside, in the gradually stilling world,
a bus has stalled, the driver
turning the engine, over and over again,
and someone's dog is barking at the noise,
guarding its phantom realm of bricks and weeds.
All over Fife, the roads
are blocked with fallen trees and stranded cars,
the tide keeps washing wreckage to the shore,
splints of timber, fishnets, broken toys.
This wind has blown for days across the fields,
so now the silence feels unnatural,
as if the storm is what we really need,
the sound of it, its small, forensic pleasures,
ribbons of silt or birchseed in the hall,
a feather on the bedroom windowsill,
and what we might discover of ourselves
and one another, as the night begins.
So much that moves around us in the dark
is ours: the smallest shiver in the hedge
a knowledge we have waited years to learn,
and something come inside, in that one
moment, when you hold the door ajar,
more than a gust of rain, more than the wind,
more than the Halloween ghosts we might imagine.

Those animals that figure on the walls,
those creatures we imagine on the stairs
are real, and we must give them shapes and names,
feed them with blood and salt, fix them a bed,
make shift, make good, allow them this possession.

VIII BEHOLDING

As morning moves in from the firth
I'm sitting up awake, a mug of tea
fogging the window, the bones of my hands and face
shot with insomnia's delicate, lukewarm needles.
You're still asleep. Your hair is the colour of whey
and your hand on the pillow is clenched, like a baby's fist
on a figment of heat, or whatever you've clutched in a dream,
and I suddenly want to ask
your forgiveness, for something deliberately
cruel in the way I see, in the way
all seeing could become: too hard, too clear,
refusing to find something more than the cool of morning.
It's Halloween; if only because the dead
will come all afternoon to walk the streets
in faded hats and 1950s coats,
or gather by the harbour after dark
watching for lights beyond the lights we know,
their eyes like the eyes of seals, their faces
meltwater blue, as if they had surfaced through ice,
I want to go outside and gather
buckets of rain-washed apples, scabs of leaf,
a handful of broken coal, or a yellowed stump
of spindlewood, to feed the kitchen fire,
then watch, as it dwindles to ash
by late afternoon;
or wander all day in the kirkyard, reading the names
on strangers' graves: their plots laid side by side
with those they loved and hated, those they feared;
friends who betrayed them; children who watched them die.
It's what they meant by coming to this place
and choosing to remain, though decades fastened their hands
to kindling and wire, and the dampness that seeped through the walls
all winter long.

        Now, suddenly, you're talking in your sleep,
your face on the pillow like one of those paper masks
we used to make in school, for Halloween,
talking to someone you've dreamed, while your white hands
fasten on something fragile or easily lost,
a strand of hair, a ring, a stranger's arm,
the promise you have to remember, that brings us home.

PENITENCE

I was driving into the wind
on a northern road,
the redwoods swaying around me like a black
ocean.
       I'd drifted off: I didn't see the deer
till it bounced away,
the back legs swinging outwards as I braked
and swerved into the tinder
of the verge.
             Soon as I stopped
the headlamps filled with moths
and something beyond the trees was tuning in,
a hard attention
boring through my flesh
to stroke the bone.
                That shudder took so long
to end, I thought the animal had slipped
beneath the wheels, and lay there
quivering.
        I left the engine running; stepped outside;
away, at the edge of the light, a body
shifted amongst the leaves
and I wanted to go, to help, to make it well,
but every step I took
pushed it away.
            Or – no; that's not the truth,
or all the truth:
now I admit my own fear held me back,
not fear of the dark, or that presence
bending the trees;
not even fear, exactly, but the dread
of touching, of colliding with that pain.
I stood there, in the river of the wind,

for minutes; then I walked back to the car
and drove away.
             I want to think that deer
survived; or, if it died,
it slipped into the blackness unawares.
But now and then I drive out to the woods
and park the car: the headlamps fill with moths;
the woods tune in; I listen to the night
and hear an echo, fading through the trees,
my own flesh in the body of the deer
still resonant, remembered through the fender.

PORTS

'Pas de port. Ports inconnus.'
Henri Michaux

I HAVEN

Our dwelling place:
                the light above the firth
shipping forecasts
        gossip
                theorems

the choice of a single word to describe
the gun-metal grey of the sky
                    as the gulls
flicker between the roofs
on Tolbooth Wynd.

            Whenever we think of home
we come to this:
the handful of birds and plants we know by name
rain on the fishmonger's window
                      the walleyed plaice
freckled with spots
        the colour of orangeade.

We look for the sifted light
that settles around the salvaged
hull of the *Research*
            perched on its metal stocks
by the harbour wall

its smashed keel half-restored
                the workmen

caged in a narrow scaffold
                              matching the ghosts
of umber and *blanc-de-Chine*.

We notice how dark it is
                              a dwelling place
for something in ourselves that understands

the beauty of wreckage
                              the beauty
of things submerged

II URLICHT

                      – our
dwelling place:
                a catalogue of wrecks
and slants of light –

never the farmsteader's vision
of angels
        his wayside shrines
to martyrs and recent saints
                              the rain
gleaming on wrapped chrysanthemums
                                      forced
roses and pinks –

here we have nothing to go on
                                or nothing more
than light and fog
                a shiver in the wind
or how the sky can empty all at once
when something like music comes
                                or rather

something like the gap between a sound
and silence
             like the ceasing of a bell

or like the noise a tank makes as it fills
and overflows.

              How everyone expects
that moment when a borrowed motor stalls
half-way across the channel
                         and you sit
quiet
     amazed by the light
                        aware
of everything
             aware of shoals and stars
shifting around you
                   endlessly

entwined.
         Our neighbour
                      John
who spends his free time diving

plumbing the sea for evidence and spilt
cargoes
       who has burrowed in the mud
to touch the mystery of something absolute

can tell you how
                out in the Falklands
he walked inland
climbing a slope where blown sand turned to grass
the emptiness over his head
like a form of song.

He still has the pictures he took
                            of backward glances
of whale bones on the shore
                         the wind exact
and plaintive in the whited vertebrae.

He'd been out diving
                       finding the shallow wrecks
of coalships from Wales
                     and one old German
sail-boat
     whose quick-thinking crew
had scuppered it just offshore
to douse a fire:

a cargo of beer and gunpowder
still in the hold
each stoppered bottle
sealed with water weed.

                     He'd walked less than a mile
when
    settled upon its haunches
                        as if it had recently
stopped to rest

he found a carcass: one of those feral
cattle that wander the dunes
                        a long-forgotten
ghost of husbandry.

It might have been there for years
                          but it looked alive
the way it had been preserved
in the cold dry air

and he stood in the wind to listen
                               as if he might hear
radio in the horns
             or ancient voices
hanging in the vacuum of the skull.

He had his camera
             but couldn't take
the picture he wanted
               the one he thinks of now
as perfect
      – he couldn't betray
that animal silence
               the threadwork of grass through the hide
the dwelling place
             inherent in the spine

                              that

III MOORINGS

kinship of flesh with flesh.

                  When we go walking
early
    at the furled edge of the sea

we find dark webs of crabmeat
                      herring-bone
                            wet
diaphragms of stranded jellyfish

spring water mingles with salt beneath the church
where Anstruther's dead are harboured in silent loam

sea-litter washes the wall where the graveyard ends
a scatter of shells and hairweed
                                          and pebbles of glass
made smooth
            in the sway of the tide.

From here
            amongst the angel-headed stones
we see the town entire:
                      the shiplike kirk
the snooker hall above the library

the gift-shop on the corner
                              windows packed
with trinkets of glass
                and pictures of towns like this

a rabble of gulls
            the scarlet and cherry red
of lifebelts and cars
                the bus that will wait by the dock
for minutes
        before it returns
to Leven.

        By evening the harbour belongs
to men at work.
They're swaddled in orange or lime-green
overalls
      their faces sheathed
in perspex: crouched to the blue
of their torches
                they are innocent
of presence
            flashes and sparks

dancing in the blackness of their masks
as if in emptiness.

Sometimes we stand in the cold
and watch them for hours
                          – the way
they bend into their flames
like celebrants
                immune to everything
that moves or falls around them
                                isolates
suspended in the constancy
of fire.
     This time of year
it's night by five o'clock
and as we walk
                we harbour something new:
                              the old pain
neutral and stilled in our blood
like a shipwreck observed from a distance
                              or one of those
underwater shapes we sometimes glimpse
through hairweed and clouded sand
                        a shifting form
that catches the eye for a moment
then disappears.

At dusk
      above the street
                  above the painted
shopfronts and roofs
and children walking home in twos and threes
it starts to snow.
                At one end of the quay
a boat is docked

– it's mostly fishing vessels here
        but this
is tusk-white
    with a terracotta keel
a pleasure boat
      a hope pursued through years
of casual loss.

It's unattended now
       but you could guess
its owner from the writing on the hull
a stencilled row of characters that spell
against the painted wood
        the word
S E R E N I T Y.

In daylight it would seem
almost absurd:
too sentimental
    gauche
       inaccurate
a weekend sailor's image of the sea

but now
   as snow descends into the rings
of torchlight
     and the sky above the harbour
darkens
   it is only what it seems:

a name for something wanted
        and believed

no more or less correct than anything
we use to make a dwelling in the world.

SETTLEMENTS

'God answers our prayers by refusing them.'
                                          Luther

I A PLACE BY THE SEA

Because what we think of as home
is a hazard to others
our shorelines edged with rocks and shallow
sandbanks
          reefs
where navigation fails

we mark the harbour out
with lights and noise:
flickers of green and scarlet in the dark
the long moan of a foghorn
                            when the daylight
thickens and stills

and even when we speak of other things
our prayers include all ships
                              all those at sea
navigators   pilots   lobster-crews
the man who is yanked overboard
on a line of creels
whole families of boys and quiet fathers
lost in a sudden squall
                        a mile from land.

It's not that we surrender to our fear
or trust in nothing
it's just that the darkness
opens
      on mornings like this

filling with distance and starlight for mile after mile
when we wake to the taste of milk
                                  and the scent of coal
in rooms bequeathed to us by merchantmen
who stocked the roof with powders
                                  sacks of grain
spicetree and crumbs of saffron

it's not that we are lost
or far from home

it's just that the world
seems strange
        on nights like this

when we lie with the ghosts of ourselves
                                  – these habitual flavours:
aloe and eau-de-cologne
                and the ribbon of sweetness
that stays on my hands for hours
when I turn
        to sleep

II FISHERFOLK AT NEWHAVEN
after Hill and Adamson

Mending their nets
        or standing in their dim
smoke houses
        hearing the water
slap against the wood-face of the dock

and thinking of nights at sea
                            of a spilt
quiver of brindled fish
on the slur of the deck

of calling back and forth through lanternlight
for uncles and second cousins
to come and look:

the fruits of the ocean
                              tarred with a difficult blue
as they haul them in
siren faces poised
                as if to speak

but silent
        like the wives they leave behind
for weeks and months
                          beguiled by the wounded skins
they bring in from the dark
                        the slatted crates

dripping with salt and copper
                          and the pale
shimmer of phosphorescence
                        like the chill
that grows between their hands
                        on chapel days.

III WELL

There's more to it than I thought –
more than the house, or our stilled bed
when no one is here,

the book you have left face down
on the kitchen table,
the tangle of hair in the brush, the litter of clothes
– there's more to the making of home
than I ever expected:
a process of excavation, of finding
something in myself to set against
the chill of the other,
the echo you do not hear, when I stop to listen,
the stranger who wakes in the dark from a fetid dream
of ditches and milt;
and how we go on digging when it seems
there's nothing else to find – or nothing more
than ghosts and unanswered prayers –
is part of it, though not the better part
we hoped for: it's the old need
keeps us strong.
So when I turn to say, at times like this,
that something else is with us all along
I'm thinking of that woman in the town
who told me how she worked all afternoon,
she and her husband digging in the heat, bees
drifting back and forth through currant stands,
the sound of their breathing
meshed with the weave and spin
of swallows:
how, after an hour, they struck on an unexpected
flagstone of granite
and lifted the lid on a coal-black
circle of fresh spring water under the stone,
leaning in hard for the earth-smell of last year's fruit
then sweetness, surprising as rain, or bittern-calls,
rising like a slow, unfurling shoot
of asphodel.
                    It's what I think of now

as home: that wellspring
deep beneath the house
they tasted for an hour, then put away,
sliding the cover back, and coming in
to all they knew, immersed in the quiet purr
of radio, those voices from the air
bleeding in through swallow-songs and bees
to make them plausible again, though they had touched
what turns to black; the sifted heart of matter.

IV WHAT WE KNOW OF HOUSES

Sunday
    We are driving to the woods
to find the hidden origin of rain:
a shallow basin carved into the rock
where Pictish chiefs assembled with their kin
to reinvent the world
                   – or so we say –
though no one knows for sure who gathered here
or why.

    I like to think of them
on days like this
perched on a shelf of rock beneath the trees
watching their children
                  thinking of their stock
then stepping out
             to sacrifice
                      or blessing
as we have stood together in the shade
made awkward by the quiet of the place
a darkness that continues while the sun
brightens the fields

                        and gardens fill with light
in market towns or tidy golf-hotels
above the sea.

Though nothing here is sacred
                                – not to us –
even the pool of water stopped with leaves
the carvings in the rock
                        the standing stone
are set apart

and nothing we can touch or say will bring us
closer to the spirit of the place.
Our holy ground is barely recognised:
unverified
            an atmospheric trick
a common miracle that finds us out
alone in attic rooms
                        as spring begins:
a rhythm in the light
                        a line of song
the sudden taste of grass
                        high in the roof
wind through the gaps in the beams
                                the rafters spiced
with cumin
and the aftertaste of nets

and all along the roads
                        where dry-stone walls
have toppled
            and the steady gorse digs in
embers of perfume, sealed in a crown of thorns:

unseasonable   stubborn   everyday

– it's bright as the notion of home:
                              not something held
or given
       but the painful gravity
that comes of being settled on the earth
redeemable   inventive   inexact
and capable of holding what we love
in common
           making good
with work and celebration
                         charged
to go out unprepared into the world

and take our place for granted
                         every time
we drive back through the slowly dimming fields
to quiet rooms
              and prayers that stay unanswered.

THE ASYLUM DANCE

for Dag Andersson

At one time, I looked forward to the dance:
wandering back and forth in the quiet
heat of an August morning,
packing the car with cup cakes and lemonade,
boxes of plums or cherries, petits-fours,
nuts and spice cake, mousse and vol-au-vents.
At noon I would go upstairs
to wash and change
– Sunday best, a clean white shirt and tie –
while mother made her face
and fixed her hair.
It was something we did, every year,
in that backwater town,
abandoning our lawns and flower beds,
to meet the patients, out at Summerswood.
It seemed a privilege to be allowed
within those gates, and know we might return,
to see the meadows, striped with light and shade,
the silent lake, the fallen cedar trees.
We went there for the dance: a ritual
of touch and distance, webs of courtesy
and guesswork; shifts
from sunlight into shade;
and when the patients came downstairs
to join us, smiling, utterly polite,
in new-pressed clothes, like cousins twice-removed,
they had the look of people glimpsed in mirrors,
subtle as ghosts, yet real, with the vague
good-humour of the lost.
How we appeared to them, I can only imagine:
too solid, perhaps, too easy with ourselves,

sure of our movements, blessed with a measured desire.
All afternoon we picnicked on the lawn
then danced in awkward couples to the hiss
of gramophones, as daylight turned to dusk;
a subtle exchange in the half-light; acts of grace:
townsfolk conferring the weight of a normal world,
homes in the suburbs, the brisk lives of men who can sleep,
the practised charm of women who believe,
who wake and forget what they dreamed, and go off to
   work,
and wish for nothing.
Beside the patients, we were lithe and calm:
we doled out charity and easy praise
and waited for the dancing to erase
the pain in the knot of the throat, the birdlike
angle of defeat against the spine.
We loved them for the way they witnessed us,
standing in twos and threes in the waning light,
made other by the rhythm of the dance,
the pull of a larger world, and that taste on the air
of birch-woods and streams: that knowledge of ourselves
as bodies clothed in brightness, moving apart
and coming together, cooling
slowly, as the lawns and rose-beds cooled,
heat seeping out from the skin and bleeding away,
the goldenrod turning to smoke
at the fence line.
Friendships began out there, to be resumed
year after year, the difficult months between
absolved by the summer light; and once,
a love affair, of sorts: an awkward boy
finding a girl, and leading her, mock-unwilling
into the lighted circle of the dance, to venture steps
that felt like steps on ice, the floorboards
creaking, and thin as paper.

They danced less than an hour, then she was gone,
and when he went back, next morning, the nurses
turned him away.
I think of her every day, I dream her skin,
and for years I have driven out, in the August heat,
alone now, with Mother gone, and my contributions
store-bought: jars of pickles; cling-wrapped bread.
I stand by myself, excused from the solid ring
of bodies and, for minutes at a time,
I see it all from somewhere far above,
some landing in the house, some upper room:
it makes me think of pictures I have seen
of dancers – wisps of movement on a lawn
at sunset: faces muffled, bodies twined;
the figures so close to the darkness, they might be
apparitions, venturing on form,
pinewoods above the lake, a suggestion of watchers,
a gap between night and day, between light and shade,
and faces melting, one into the next
as if they were all one flesh, in a single dream,
and nothing to make them true, but space, and time.

FIELDS

'From my rotting body, flowers shall grow and I am in them and that is eternity.'

Edvard Munch

I LANDFILL

In ways the dead are placed
                       or how
they come to rest

I recognise myself
                  insomniac
                           arms
angled
   or crossed:

children in skullcaps
soldiers with hob-nailed boots
or sandals placed like gifts
beside their feet

priests at the gates of death
                           or afterlife
their vestments stained with malt
and carbon
        fingers rinsed
with camomile
            or honeyed meadowsweet

resemble me
         laid sleepless by your side
as if there were something else
                          some chore or rite
to be accomplished.

                        Once
in rural Fife
            and Angus
                        farmers held
one acre of their land
                untilled
                        unscarred
to house this mute
concurrence with the dead
choosing from all their fields
one empty plot
that smelled or tasted right
                        one house of dreams.

They walled it in
and called it Gude Man's Land
                        or Devil's Piece

and some would say they guessed well every time
knowing the gist of the thing
                        the black in the green
of stitchwort.
            Though I can't believe they thought
that tremor in the grass on windless days
was devil's work:
                yet
where they found old bones
                        or spills of blood
where birdsong ceased
and darkness stayed till noon
they recognised some kinship with the dead
with bodies they had found
                        in nether fields
the faces soft
            still lifelike
                        grass and roots

decaying in the gut.
They guessed it well
                divined its mysteries
and left it to the pipistrelles
and jays.

When I was five
or six
     – I can't recall –
the land for miles was sick with foot and mouth

and grateful for the work
                my father
travelled the length of the county
                        digging pits
for slaughtered herds.

On farm after farm for miles
                    in the paling light
he worked all day
         and far into the dusk
then caught the last bus home
                    his shirtsleeves stitched
with quicklime and dust.

That was the year our neighbour
                    Agnes
                        died:
her body thick with growth
                the blackness
tight between her lips
like needlework.

I thought she had been touched by foot and mouth:
a fog of disease that spread

                              on our spoons and knives
and bottles in the playground
stopped with cream

and I waited for my father to begin
unravelling
          like twine.

I stood in the kitchen and watched
                                    while my mother
fixed him his tea
amazed at how lonely he looked
                              how suddenly tired
a blur of unspoken hurt
on his mouth and eyes

and I loitered all afternoon
                              while friends and strangers
emptied the house our neighbour had kept intact
and still as a church.

They worked all day
                    intent and businesslike
clearing the rooms
                the wardrobes
                                    the silent cupboards
folding her winter coats and summer shawls
packing her shoes in boxes
                          her letters
                                      her make-up
and bearing it away
                  to other rooms
timesoiled
          infected.

I scarcely recall:
         there was something I overheard
a sense of the ditch
            and the blind calves laid in the earth
a nightmare for weeks
of gunshots
       and buried flesh

yet still
       when I lie naked in our bed
I sense my father waiting
                  and I shift
like someone in a dream
              so he will turn
and go back to the fire
            and let me rest.

II TWO GARDENS

When we came it was couch-grass and brambles,
colonies of rue amongst the thorns,
a leafless shrub that smelt of creosote
and simmered in the heat.
I liked it then. I liked its stillnesses:
the ruined glasshouse packed with honey-vine,
the veins of ash, the pools of fetid rain.
Sometimes we found strange droppings by the hedge:
badger or fox, you said; but the scent was laced
with citrus, and I kept imagining
a soft-boned creature stalled beneath the shed,
strayed from its purpose, wrapped in musk and spines.
In spring we set to work; we marked our bounds
and found the blueprint hidden in the weeds,
implicit beds, the notion of a pond.
You sifted out the shards of porcelain,

illumined willows, scraps of crescent moon;
I gathered clinker, labels, half a set
of Lego.
        As I watched that summer's fires
I wondered what was burning: living bone,
pockets of silk and resin, eggs and spawn,
and, afterwards, I saw what we had lost:
surrendered to our use, inanimate,
the land was measured out in bricks and twine,
a barbecue, a limestone patio.
The work is finished now; but after dark
I feel the creatures shivering away,
abandoning an absence we accept
as natural: the unexpectant trees;
the silence where the blackbird vanishes.
At times the ghosts are almost visible
between our trellises and folding chairs:
just as old harbours sometimes reappear
through fog or rain, or market towns dissolve
to gift us with a dusk of shining air,
the garden we destroyed is almost here,
nothing but hints and traces, nothing known,
but something I have wanted all along:
a thread of pitchblende, bleeding through a stone,
or snow all morning, cancelling the lawn.

III GUDE MAN'S LAND

There was something I wanted to find,
coming home late in the dark, my fingers
studded with clay,
oak-flowers caught in my hair, the folds of my jacket
busy with aphids.
I slept in my working clothes

and walked out in the buttermilk of dawn
to start again.
Sometimes I turned and saw him through the leaves,
a face like mine, but empty of desire,
pure mockery, precision of intent,
a poacher's guile, a butcher's casual charm.
The house filled slowly with the evidence
I carried home: old metals, twisted roots,
bottles of silt and water, scraps of cloth.
My neighbours passed me on the road to kirk
and thought me mad, no doubt, though I could see
their omnipresent God was neither
here nor there.
Who blurred the sheep with scab? Who curdled milk?
Who was it fledged the wombs of speechless girls?
They knew, and made their standard offerings
and called it peace. But he was with them still.
His secret thoughts were written in their veins,
and when they dreamed of music, it was his,
and when I dreamed, I fed him in the dark,
wifeless and quiet, lacking in conversation.
He knew what I wanted; I knew what I would not dare;
lying alone in the darkness, burning with fever,
walking the fields in the rain, at home and lost,
the feel of his recent warmth
on the tips of my fingers,
the taste of his body minted in the wild
patches of grass that quickened along the walls
or ran in circles round the nether field,
absorbing the daylight,
informing the guesswork of children.

IV OTHERLIFE

Be quick when you switch on the light
and you'll see the dark
was how my father put it:
                              catch
the otherlife of things
                       before a look
immerses them.
                 Be quick
and you'll see the devil at your back
and he'd grin
                as he stood in the garden
– cleaning his mower
                          wiping each blade in turn
with a cotton rag
the pulped grass and bright-green liquor
staining his thumbnails
and knuckles.
                He always seemed
transfigured by the work
glad of his body's warmth
                           and the smell
of aftermath.
He'd smoke behind the shed
                         or dart
for shelter under the eaves
                       the fag-end
cradled in his hand
against the rain:

a man in an old white shirt
                     a pair of jeans
some workboots he'd bought for a job
that was never completed.
                    And later
                            after he died

I buried those clothes in a field above the town
finding a disused lair amongst the stones
that tasted of water
                      then moss
                                then something
sharper
      like a struck match in the grass
or how he once had smelled
                            home from the pit
his body doused in gas
                    and anthracite.

I still remember
                  somewhere in the flesh
asleep and waking
                  how the body looked
that I had made
the empty shirt and jeans
                        the hobnailed boots
and how I sat for hours
                  in that wet den
where something should have changed
                              as skin and bone
are altered
        and a new life burrows free
– sloughed from a slurry of egg-yolk
                              or matted leaves
gifted with absence
                speaking a different tongue –
but all I found in there was mould and spoor
where something had crept away
                      to feed
                              or die
or all I can tell
                though for years I have sat up late

and thought of something more
                                  some half-seen thing
the pull of the withheld
                  the foreign joy
I tasted that one afternoon
                       and left behind
when I made my way back down the hill
with the known world about me.

HUSBANDRY

Why children make pulp of slugs
with a sprinkling of salt

or hang a nest of fledglings on a gate
with stolen pins

is why I sometimes turn towards the dark
and leave you guessing,

only to know the butter and nickel taste
of cruelty;
        to watch, and show no sign

of having seen.
           Not
wickedness, that sometimes celebrates

a tightness in the mind;
but what I comprehend

of fear and love:
cradled remoteness, nurtured by stalled desire;

willed deprivation;
the silence I'm learning by heart.

ROADS

'Transcurrir es suficiente,
             Transcurrir es quedarse.'
                          Octavio Paz

I DRIVING TO MIRTIOTISSA

We learned to avoid the village
to drive through the olive groves
                          evading
children and dogs
             and old men with sodden voices
calling to one another through the trees

the way we avoided noon
                   or the sickening
halt of the butcher's doorway
leaving the white-hot streets and the slide of traffic
islands of rubble
             flashes of broken glass
oil-slicks and fruit-spills
                   the sudden
untenable light

cruising the dirt-roads and alleys
on blue afternoons
for something we almost found
again and again:

a sand-lizard perched on a rock or a clump of thorns
the fretwork between its fingers
                          the fire-coloured throat
the spiders in the gaps between the rocks
goats in the weeds
             their slack mouths and sun-bleared eyes

remembering panic
                that faint trace of shit and vanilla
that hangs in the shade.

You were reading a book about angels
the way they appear on the road to the unsuspecting
wingless
      yet ringed with light
                          they could pass
for locals:
      men in boots and cotton shirts
a girl in a printed dress
                beside a well

and though we imagined
we couldn't believe in such things
if anything was there
            in that black light
we knew it would be lost
                in no man's land

on back-roads scabbed with weeds or veiled with sand
running through chicken farms and unmapped towns
or rising to the chill
of native pine:

angels
    or Pan
— that god of sudden absence
come from the shadows to meet you
                                  a hairsbreadth away
a blackness in the everyday event
like something tethered

a flock of birds descending on the church
a spill of figs
    the unexpected chill
of spice-haunted wells
or miles of cicadas
     stopped
in the noontime lull

though we guessed that the angel of roads
or the panic of standstills
was less than the weight of ourselves
being lost or found
     and even this a story
        like

II KIDNAPPED

that story of our exile in the hills
months of pursuit
    the roads whiting out in the dark
fresh disappearances
    spotting the matted grass

— they were still on my scent
though I'd crossed those mountain streams
a dozen times

the water filling my boots
the year-long cold
seeping through my bones to fledge the groin

and I'm travelling still: my name on a borrowed passport
sleeping between the graves in an upland church
foraging for eggs and spills of grain

living caesura, less than the sum of my parts
I'm waiting for the limbo of a life
that goes without saying:

a circle in the woods of mint and coal
where someone has stopped before now
to light a fire

        – almost
but not quite right:
illusion
    like the one who stays at home
lost in the warmth of butter and cherry tea
and wanting for nothing
                  immune to the smell of fairgrounds:
illusion
    like the one who would arrive
travelling unawares
           though clues abound:
the smell of standing water
                barley mows
or alpine meadows glimpsed from the early train
to Brasov
    or Cluj

those upland silences that last for days
delectable mountains
              hillsides clad with pines
and cherries
    the grey of nearness
                    soldiers
standing in a clearing by a truck
boys from the country in jackboots
and threadbare shirts:

        illusory

III PILGRIMAGE

                        as all these journeys are:
home after dark
        on a late bus
                or waiting alone
at the station
        the platform light
suddenly all there is for miles around

and something I almost recall
                some hunting bird
skimming low over the tracks
                and vanishing.
And even if I recognise the shape
even if something remains
                some haunting call
I know from somewhere else
                – some film or tape –
even if some local perfume drifts
towards me
      as I cross the narrow bridge
an inkling of oilseed rape
              or ripened corn
the scent of orchards
        fish-meal
                rendered bone
there's nothing here to understand or claim
nothing to grasp
        nothing to think of

as true.

      I've come this way before
                I've read the maps:

the dream of a shoreline
                         the delicate upland trees
delectable mountains nuzzling the rear-view mirror
houses standing open
                      doors ajar
the windows like the gaps where angels live
in old nativities
signals above a meadow
                         porch-lights and doors
as if there were something more
to be revealed.
I have driven this road too often
                           and come too far
losing the taste for home:
                   its standing warmth
the gravities and shifts
we dwell upon

                 – so when I reach the hollow of the stairs
intruder on the dream you've shifted from

I'm glad of the silence
                  glad of the distance between us
the blackness of country roads I have smuggled in
on my shirtsleeves
             the flavour of rain
and nothingness
                – a gap you would not house
no matter how often you turn
                       with the feel
of something at your back
                     some hirsute god
some cloven-footed wisp of the angelic

       – though speaking for myself
                          I'd want to say
this nothing is why I am out on a starless road
learning the true extent of no man's land
the night wind threading my eyes
                           and nowhere to go.

IV IDA Y VUELTA
i.m. Octavio Paz

Remember that Alpujarran hill-town:
gusts of broom for miles then an arabic
scribble of burning bush amongst the stones?
The empty hostel where we lay awake
till morning, while a long-awaited rain
unmapped the streets, the gardens moored in smoke,
the tree-lined squares?
                       Remember the sullen
music of cicadas, sudden panic
in the still of afternoon? – the way
we almost learned to chance upon the air
the stain of something richer – how the stay
of terror is a gift for smaller fear:
that beast we conjured from the common day:
man-sized; inert; a ghost of teeth and hair.

                – one way to say it
perhaps

     or this: how
                leaving Frankfurt
the plane rose slowly to a wall
of thunder-cloud
                shuddering in its bones for the moment's
pause before the stillness
of a fall

then lightning over fields that bled
like the pastilles of freshened colour in a school-child's
paint-box: rapeseed yellow
                                      clover green
umber and terrasiena.

How terror is always shifting
                                between the glow
of home
          and the chill of departure

Yo atravesé los arcos y los puentes
Yo estaba vivo, en busca de la vida

and love is something learned
like dancing:
knowing the steps
but moving without desire
in a partner's arms

Yo estaba vivo y vi muchos fantasmas,
Todos de carne y hueso y todos ávidos

or how a life
can never quite be seen
in this measure of rain
a bruise of kisses
seeping to the bone
and waiting there
to flower as a word

Tigre, novilla, pulpo, yedra en llamas

whichever one you choose
it's all the same:
arrival; end; hibiscus; carbon; stone.

V ETERNAL RETURN

Yo estaba vivo y fui a buscar la muerte

– an algebra
        a science of goodbyes
somewhere beyond the absence implicit in grammar:

lost
   and
found.

The road
       or the town's last street
when they worked all afternoon to build
a fairground
       men in boots and cotton shirts
rigging a world of candy-floss and diesel
and setting it alight so I could dream
of running away
       becoming the competent son
you would never imagine.
How even now
       in dreams I have failed to confess
I stand at the edge of the woods on Fulford Road
my mind on the blue of elsewhere:
          frog-headed
vagrant
I walk to the last fuzzed streetlamp and hitch a ride
running away to the promise of freight cars in sidings
gulf-water
    wood-stoves
        disappearances.
This dream recurs
       I find it in our bed

the taste of doorways
            windows
                        exit roads
or how there are times
            coming home
when everything seems richer for my absence:
car parks around the airport
perfectly ordered
            the crowd at the gate
with labels or startled joy
for the newly arrived

our kitchen windows flushed with light and steam
and the flavour of cherry tea that has lingered for days
while I've been gone.

Stop moving
            and another life begins:
the motion the tide conceals
                        the caress of erosion
or how the beginning of autumn is quietly gloved
in August
the first bright
sugars turning to gold
in locust trees and false acacias.

I taste it on the windows in the dusk
of morning:
a perfume so close to travel I imagine
deer trails in the hills
            the white
hiatus of woodland tracks
                        or the sherbet fizz
of rock-salt and drifted sand
on a coastal highway.
How once
      driving back to my room

in Mountain View
I wanted to stop the car and disappear
to pull in under a cypress and slip away
venturing into the nowhere
of starlight and wind
and leaving no trace.

I've run like this for years
      and I've returned
– the promised no one left behind a door
or tethered to a borderline of sand
and poppies.

I've wanted so many lives
      such otherness
and so much less than anything we have:
some garden of broken stones and aquilegias
a shoal of angel fish in makeshift graves
unscheduled stops
     in no man's land
        or Tulsa

and yet
  forgive me this:
I never really mastered coming home
skilled in that childhood-for-years of travelling light

forgive me:
    I still can't resist
the sound of a fair in the distance
        the new-crushed grass
those sixties songs
    the heat of the machines
 I still can't resist the girls on the promenade
 walking the front in lipstick and brand-new hairdos

the boys from the caravan parks come out
to stand in the bars all night
                          like their father's ghosts
sullen and proud
                and as lost in the world they inherit
as stray dogs
        or mink

and forgive me
        that I cannot leave or stay
that I'm only a moment away
                      from being unseen

forgive me
        being not the man I seem
not lost or found
                but somewhere in between.

KOI

The trick is to create a world
from nothing

               – not the sound a blackbird makes
in drifted leaves

not dogwood
             or the unexpected scent
of jasmine by the west gate

                     not the clouds
reflected in these puddles all around
the bowling green
             deserted after rain
and darker than an early polaroid –

but nothing
             which is present in the flesh
as ripeness is: a lifelong urgency.

The trick is in the making
                   not the made

beginning where an idle mind spools out
to borderline and limit
             half a mile
of shadow in the pine woods
                   or a rim

of wetland – rush and willow
gathered close
             like mourners in the dark –

                         a sudden
ambiguity of liverwort or birch

suggesting no man's land
       or journey's end.

As everything is given
      and conceived
imagined real
    a stone's throw in the mind

it's not the thing itself
      but where it stands

— the shadows fanned
      or dripping from a leaf
the gap between each named form and the next

where frogs and dragonflies arrive
from nowhere
      and the kingdom is at hand
in every shift of colour and degree

bullfinch and squirrel
      hawk-moth

and antirrhinum.

All afternoon we've wandered from the pool
to alpine beds and roses
      and the freshly-painted
palm house

   all afternoon
we've come back to this shoal
of living fish.

Crimson and black
     pearl-white
        or touched with gold
the koi hang in a realm of their invention

with nothing that feels like home
                              — a concrete pool
and unfamiliar plants spotted with light
birdsong and traffic
                    pollen and motes of dust

and every time the veil above their heads
shivers into noise
                  they dart
and scatter

          though it seems more ritual now
than lifelike fear
                  as if they understood
in principle
            but couldn't wholly grasp

the vividness of loss

and every time we gaze into this pool
of bodies
         we will ask

how much they know of us
                        and whether this
is all illusion

          like the play of light
across a surface gilded with a drift
of pollen

          or the sound a blackbird makes
as it withdraws
               one moment at a time

remembering its myth of origin.

ANIMALS

for Allison Funk

There are nights when we cannot name
the animals that flit across our headlights,

even on moonlit journeys, when the road
is eerie and still

and we smell the water long before
the coast road, or those lamps across the bay,

they cross our path, unnameable and bright
as any in the sudden heat of Eden.

Mostly, it's rabbit, or fox, though we've sometimes caught
a glimpse of powder blue, or Chinese white,

or chanced upon a mystery of eyes
and passed the last few miles in wonderment.

It's like the time our only neighbour died
on Echo Road,

leaving her house unoccupied for months,
a darkness at the far end of the track

that set itself apart,
the empty stairwell brooding in the heat,

the blank rooms filling with scats
and the dreams of mice.

In time, we came to think that house contained
a presence: we could see it from the yard

shifting from room to room in the autumn rain
and we thought it was watching us: a kindred shape

more animal than ghost.
They say, if you dream an animal, it means

'the self' – that mess of memory and fear
that wants, remembers, understands, denies,

and even now, we sometimes wake from dreams
of moving from room to room, with its scent on our hands

and a slickness of musk and fur
on our sleep-washed skins,

though what I sense in this, and cannot tell
is not the continuity we understand

as self, but life, beyond the life we live
on purpose: one broad presence that proceeds

by craft and guesswork,
shadowing our love.

HEAT WAVE

After it rained, the back roads gusted with steam,
and the gardens along our street filled with the scent
of stocks and nicotiana,
but it didn't get properly hot till the night drew in,
humid and heavy as glass
on our well-kept lawn.
It was high in the summer. With everyone else
in town for the Lammas fair
I took the meadow-path to where the river
stalled on a sudden blackness: alders
shrouded in night and warmth, and the first slow owl
charting the further bank.

There was always movement there
beneath the slick of moonlight on the turning
water, like a life beneath the life
I understood as cattle tracks and birds:
a darker presence, rising from the stream,
to match my every move, my every breath.
Eel-black and cold, it melded in my flesh
with all the nooks and crannies of the world
where spawn appears, or changelings slip their skins
to ripen at the damp edge of the day,
still blurred with mud
and unrecovered song.

But that night, as the sky above me turned,
I found a different swimmer in the steady
shimmer of the tide,
a living creature, come from the other side
to slip into the cool
black water. I remember how she looked,
beneath the moon, so motiveless and white,

her body like a pod that had been shelled
and emptied: Mrs Pearce, my younger sister's
science teacher, turning in the lit
amazement of a joy that I could almost
smell, across the haze of drifting heat.

I was crouched beneath a stand
of willows and I guess she didn't see
the boy who watched her swim for half an hour
then turn for home beneath the August moon,
a half-smile on her face, her auburn hair
straggling and damp;
yet later, as I walked the usual streets,
I thought that she would stop and recognise
a fellow soul, with river in his eyes,
slipping home under a wave of light and noise,
and finding the key to her nights
in his soft, webbed fingers.

HISTORY

St Andrews: West Sands; September 2001

Today
    as we flew the kites
– the sand spinning off in ribbons along the beach
and that gasoline smell from Leuchars gusting across
the golf links;
        the tide far out
and quail-grey in the distance;
                people
jogging, or stopping to watch
as the war planes cambered and turned
in the morning light –

today
    – with the news in my mind, and the muffled dread
of what may come –

           I knelt down in the sand
with Lucas
    gathering shells
and pebbles
    finding evidence of life in all this
driftwork:
    snail shells; shreds of razorfish;
smudges of weed and flesh on tideworn stone.

At times I think what makes us who we are
is neither kinship nor our given states
but something lost between the world we own
and what we dream about behind the names

on days like this
>   our lines raised in the wind
our bodies fixed and anchored to the shore

and though we are confined by property
what tethers us to gravity and light
has most to do with distance and the shapes
we find in water
>   reading from the book
of silt and tides
>   the rose or petrol blue
of jellyfish and sea anemone
combining with a child's
first nakedness.

Sometimes I am dizzy with the fear
of losing everything – the sea, the sky,
all living creatures, forests, estuaries:
we trade so much to know the virtual
we scarcely register the drift and tug
of other bodies
>   scarcely apprehend
the moment as it happens: shifts of light
and weather
>   and the quiet, local forms
of history: the fish lodged in the tide
beyond the sands;
>   the long insomnia
of ornamental carp in public parks
captive and bright
>   and hung in their own
slow-burning
>   transitive gold;
>   jamjars of spawn
and sticklebacks

                    or goldfish carried home
from fairgrounds
              to the hum of radio

but this is the problem: how to be alive
in all this gazed-upon and cherished world
and do no harm

                a toddler on a beach
sifting wood and dried weed from the sand
and puzzled by the pattern on a shell

his parents on the dune slacks with a kite
plugged into the sky
                    all nerve and line

patient; afraid; but still, through everything
attentive to the irredeemable.

AFTER LUCRETIUS

Nam quodcumque suis mutatum finibus exit,
Continuo hoc mors est illius quod fuit ante.
                                              Lucretius

I

It happens from time to time,
on days like this

– in winter, when the air is cold
and still,

the boats at the harbour
perched on their wooden stocks,

the gaps between the houses
filled with light –

it happens that I think of all
the vanishings I learned about in childhood:

that ship they found at sea,
unanchored, blind,

the table set for lunch, the galley
filling with steam;

the blank of the lamp-room
at Flannan, where they found

no sign of the men
who were waiting to be relieved;

the boy from a northern village, going out
at daybreak, to get kindling for a fire,

a line of footprints
stopping in the woods

and gradually erased
by morning snow.

When they speak about angels in books,
I think what they mean is this sudden

arrival at somewhere else
through a rift in the fabric,

this glimpse of the absence that forms
between two lives

– and it comes as no surprise, on days like this,
alone in the house, or walking on the shore

at evening, that I'll stop dead and recall
the disappearances my childhood self

never quite engineered,
or how it is a legend in these parts

that one bright afternoon,
in wintertime,

something will come from nowhere
and touch a man

for no good reason; ice-cold on his skin
or sharp as a needle,

it finds him and moves away
and leaves no mark.

It's not what he expected, neither death
nor absolution, but a slow and painless

fall between the collarbone and wrist
that lasts for days,

and when he disappears,
amidst the thaw,

there is nothing to show he is missing,
not even

II

    an absence.

Though each thing dies
into its own becoming,
the shed skin falling away,
still beautiful:

an empty form,
but governed by the moon,
like bone,
or thaw;

and if we are the fleshed
and perishable shadows of a soul
that shifts and slides
beneath this everyday

appearance, we are bound
by greenness and decay to see ourselves
each in the other, staying
and turning aside,

as lovers do, unable to resist
this ebb and flow:
new animals, with nothing in their minds
but light and air,

the creatures
of a sudden mystery,
who hurry on
towards the difficult;

III

though never the plural:
                         high barns filled with straw
and the flicker of errant birds
amongst the rafters,

a quiet fish-house, open to the sun,
where the packers sit turned from their work
to smoke or talk,

a litter of gut and ice
on the wet stone floor
catching the light,

or any schoolyard where the children wheel
and turn from their games
as if catching a sound in the distance

and waiting to hear it swell, to make it out:
a noise like water, say,
or gathered birds

far in the almost-heard, in the almost known,
is where it happens, singular and large
and unremarkable, like ice, or fire.

IV

Thirteen months of driving back and forth
across the sound:

the old reds and gunpowder blues
of tethered boats

or long-legged waders
stepping away through the mist

remembered as something
platonic.
        What we know

is never quite the sum
of what we find,

moving towards a light
we only half

imagine: salt-dreams
printed in the flesh,

the echo of other bodies we have borne
through blizzards, silence, unrequited loves

and always that foreign self, who never leaves
the middle-ground

yet never fully
hoves into view:

a blur at the edge of the print,
that might be human:

a single
time-lapsed suggestion

of movement, that could just as easily
be something else:

a litter of rags, perhaps,
or a tended fire,

and just as we see the differing
versions of grey in the offing

as woodsmoke, or the unexpected gap
where nothing happening becomes

the drama, so we find
no space for Icarus to fall

and vanish
at the blue edge of the world,

only the usual story of some
local, who went out one afternoon

and strayed home decades later, much the same
as when he left: a story with a point

you couldn't miss,
or so it would appear,

living amongst your kind
in towns like this,

where truth is always local, like the thought
that comes to mind, as winter closes in,

a thought you guard against for years
until you guess

that nothing matters less
than being seen.

THE GOOD NEIGHBOUR

Somewhere along this street, unknown to me,
behind a maze of apple trees and stars,
he rises in the small hours, finds a book
and settles at a window or a desk
to see the morning in, alone for once,
unnamed, unburdened, happy in himself.

I don't know who he is; I've never met him
walking to the fish-house, or the bank,
and yet I think of him, on nights like these,
waking alone in my own house, my other neighbours
quiet in their beds, like drowsing flies.

He watches what I watch, tastes what I taste:
on winter nights, the snow; in summer, sky.
He listens for the bird lines in the clouds
and, like that ghost companion in the old
explorers' tales, that phantom in the sleet,
fifth in a party of four, he's not quite there,
but not quite inexistent, nonetheless;

and when he lays his book down, checks the hour
and fills a kettle, something hooded stops,
as cell by cell, a heartbeat at a time,
my one good neighbour sets himself aside,
and alters into someone I have known:
a passing stranger on the road to grief,
husband and father; rich man; poor man; thief.

HAAR

Matthew 19–22

This is as good as it gets:
this cold fog over the water, this pale
companion to the dreams I can't forget
and never quite recall.

Stale afternoon. My neighbour stands in her yard
and watches the sky:
her children are gone; her husband is lost at sea;
how she remembers them now is by looking out patterns

for Arran sweaters, mittens,
balaclavas. Her landlord, a lickspittle spiv
in a flat tweed cap,
sits in his house on Toll Road

counting his money.
He's not really sure what it's for,
and he's mostly past caring
– maybe he knew something once, and maybe he woke

in the small of the dark with a glimmer of scent on his
    hands
that he couldn't quite place.
Now he's alone with his ledger.
He won't have a cat.

All day, the harbour dwindles.
Nothing much happens; there's nothing to smell or touch,
the shore road is mostly gift shops and fish'n'chips,
a colourless tavern, the glister of handmade toffees.

There are day trips out to the island, to see the puffins;

fairground attractions; amusements; a tidy marina;
boys in their hot-cars, waiting for someone to see them;
fishermen; coaches; pleasure boats; tailored poodles.

It's warmer at night, when the lights go on in the pool hall,
the moon on the empty firth like the spirit of neon,
girls from the Glasgow Fair drifting down to The Ship
for vodka and cranberry, Budweiser, rum and black,

but days are best: these days of salt and fog,
mornings when last night's dreams fit snug in my head,
erotic and golden, the clue to a better life
than this fudged and elaborate pact with a stranger's daytime.

The old town is gone.
The high sails out on the water,
boatloads of herring
gutted and trimmed on the pier,

the marriage feasts of skate
– to bring forth children –
the dead in their box-beds,
whispering under the eaves.

Now, as the haar comes in,
I look for ghosts,
children with dip-nets, women with salt in their faces,
men going out before dawn in the coats that will drown
    them,

but this is as good as it gets: this quiet fog,
the cool of it threading my eyes
with the promise of elsewhere,
its breath on my skin like the lover I meet in a dream.

My neighbour stands in her yard and stares at the sea;
her landlord drifts in a stupor of calculation;
the town hall opens for bingo; the harbour whitens;
foghorns call from the firth, like abandoned cattle;

and as I walk back from town with the milk and a paper,
the haar whites out the main streets, one by one:
James Street, John Street, Burnside, Tollbooth Wynd,
one step ahead all the time, as I make my way home,

tracing a path of erasure back to the house
where all I possess is laid up, like a storm:
my furniture, my books, my ornaments,
my lost love in the kitchen, brewing tea.

HOMAGE TO KÅRE KIVIJÄRVI

The third flight in twenty-four hours.
Travelling over flow-land, night setting in,
each scatter of light in the darkness a tentative gold
that, somewhere else,
is desk-lamp; headlights; home.

Behind me, a sunset recurs
again and again:
rose-grey, permanganate, cinnabar, mother of pearl;
ahead, a thousand miles of rocks and snow;

but what I picture, staring through the dark,
is someone in a narrow coastal town
– that string of lights against the naked sea –
a man, perhaps, beneath a yellow bulb,
in some old store room, working on a clock,

or taking a chainsaw apart, with everyday skill
and patience: a man in faded middle-age
who knows a thing or two, but rarely talks

and when he does, his voice is dark and slow,
like water lapping at a wooden dock,
more sound than sense, but none the worse for that,

with darkness all around him like a veil
and someone calling, from the kitchen door
– his wife, his daughter, standing in the light
I see from far above – to say it's time
to stop for now, to come inside and eat,

her voice half-heard, as something overhead
– a splash of light against the wavering sky –
drones through the clouds, mechanical, bereft.

THE LAST MAN TO SPEAK UBYKH*

At times, in those last few months,
he would think of a word
and he had to remember the tree, or the species of frog,
that sound denoted:

the tree itself, or the frog, or the state of mind
and not the equivalent word in another language,
the speech that had taken his sons and the mountain light;
the graves he swept and raked; the wedding songs.

While years of silence gathered in the heat,
he stood in his yard
and whispered the name of a bird
in his mother tongue,

while memories of snow and market days,
his father's hands, the smell of tamarind
receded in the names no longer used:
the blue of childhood folded like a sheet

and tucked away.
Nothing he said was remembered; nothing he did
was fact or legend
in the village square,

---

*The linguist Ole Stig Andersen was keen to seek out the remaining traces of a West Caucasian language called Ubykh. Having heard that there was one remaining speaker he set out to find the man and arrived in his village on October 8, 1992. Unfortunately, the man, Tevfik Esenc, had died a few hours earlier.

yet later they would memorise the word
he spoke that morning, just before he died:
a name for death, perhaps,
or meadow grass,

or swimming to the surface of his mind,
another word they had, when he was young,
a word they rarely spoke, though it was there
for all they knew that nobody remembered.

THE PAINTER FABRITIUS BEGINS
WORK ON THE LOST
NOLI ME TANGERE OF 1652

I

This is the myth we chose to do without;
and surely the painter imagined the garden he shows
as blue-green and mandarin – the improbable fruits
and blossoms; the patient birds;
the held breath of the shade –

surely he imagined it
with no one in the foreground but himself:
a scene from childhood, say, or early love; a moment's
homesick reinvention, not quite true, and yet
more trusted than the authorised account.

It seems so much a pretext for the real:
that dove in the upper branches, that wisp of cloud,
those children in the distance playing quoits
or calling out from one hedge to the next
the only names they know in all the world.

It seems so much a pretext for the given:
less gospel than the brilliant commonplace
of all we take for granted, vines and thorns
and morning dew receding in the grass;
that gold light in a stand of tamarisk; woman and man

arriving at this moment, not by chance,
and not quite by design, their puzzlement
the first step in a lifelong discipline
of knowing what they can and cannot touch,
what goes unspoken and what must be told:

a local sound – though everything is one –
the smell of hyacinths, a veil of bees
the closed wound and the healed: this

II

                              afterlife.

The woman cannot speak. She has no words.
Nothing she sees is true until a man
confirms her story; not one man, but four,
when giving evidence before a judge:
a man to echo everything she says,
a man to write it down and make it holy.

So what we hear is always second-hand:
as one man tells another of a scene
he never witnessed, spelling out in words
the mysteries of touch and nothingness
– and this is what we choose to do without
this testimony: upright men and true
speaking an authorised version: sexless; untouched.

They misunderstand what she says.
                              They make it new;
retell it for the version they will write
as gospel, passed from one mouth to the next
till something whole and vivid has emerged:
the empty shroud; the angel in the tomb
the resurrected man so like himself
his twin could dip three fingers in the wound
to feel the warmth – and all she memorised,
retold in altered form, is true enough;
if anything is true that can be told
when so much of the whole has been omitted.

III

The painting says the dead cannot be touched;
nothing is carried over, nothing is held,

even the people we love must steal away
in other guises: shadows in the dust

or something gone adrift between the trees,
lost in the wind, or the light of transmigration

– and this is how the spirit brings itself
to step aside: a gift to the unknown

since life itself is seamless and entire
tendon and bone remembering decay

as seeds remember trees, eggs conjure flight.
The real unmakes itself in every hand

that reaches out to touch and grasps thin air:
that newborn stranger hurrying away

to other facts, unhindered by desire
this wisp of smoke
      this song
          this tilt of bells.

IV

The painter cares for nothing but the light:
the patterns he knows; the shapes of this
commonplace magic; acres of grass,
or the shadows in a stand of citrus trees
between this moment and the middle ground.

This is his single chance to catch a glimpse
of how the soul continues, how it steps
from one life to another, almost touched
by what it leaves behind: a naked thing
the woman half-mistakes for wind, or song.

Irrational perhaps – and yet for years
he's carried in his nerves that other self
who might have come in some bright parallel,
a purer logic drawing out the form
he cradled in his chest with each held breath.

Irrational – yet what seems fixed in us
is haunted by a voice we never hear
and if the self is fixed what soul there is
is always something else, a practised craft
that ventures ounce by ounce upon its world

the way a skater ventures on to ice
one heartbeat at a time
                          – and if the self
were noun, what soul there is
is like a voice before it starts to speak

returning as they say we must return
in one form then another: cat, then bird,
then spider in the angle of the wall,
weaving a trap for flies, and at the last

the blue spark of a fly, some autumn night,
flickering out, the relict of this fire
becoming water, moonshine, flecks of dust,
time after time and each time a smaller goodbye.

V

Alone for the first time in weeks
and starting again on something he'd almost abandoned

he's thinking of the time he saw a girl
on the frost-whitened rink of the green

one hard December morning: not quite dawn
his neighbours asleep and him in a tattered coat

and slippers, in the gold cell of the attic,
brewing tea. Ghosts didn't bother him much

but this was one he'd never seen before:
a dark-haired girl in sandals and a thin white

summer dress, her head turned to the light,
the look on her face less hope than apprehension.

It took him three short steps to reach
the window: lights and shadows on the glass

becoming shapes, then absence, then the thought
of something lost before it even happened

and when he looked again, through ferns of ice,
nothing was there.

Yet now, as he sets to work in an empty room
with hours to fill, he's thinking of the time

he saw her: how he knew that he had seen
and guessed he'd been deceived, the way we guess

there's something in the world we cannot name
though each of us negotiates the form

it happens to assume: not quite the ghost
he thought he'd seen that morning while the house

was still asleep, but something he would claim
if ever it returned: half-girl; half-frost;

a resurrection waiting to begin
in flesh and bone, in touch and self-forgetting.